AF316695

Mountains and the Moon

Mountains and the Moon

STEPHEN FALCONER

RESOURCE *Publications* · Eugene, Oregon

MOUNTAINS AND THE MOON

Resource Publications
An Imprint of Wipf and Stock Publishers
199 W. 8th Ave., Suite 3
Eugene, OR 97401

www.wipfandstock.com

PAPERBACK ISBN: 979-8-3852-2666-5
HARDCOVER ISBN: 979-8-3852-2667-2
EBOOK ISBN: 979-8-3852-2668-9

07/16/24

Contents

CONTENTS

CONTENTS

CONTENTS

IN THE BEGINNING

There is clear sky after a squall,
midnight and stellar abundance fused with soil,
fetal plasma
and dew soaking moss with morning effulgence

a wish
to abandon contraction
from the moist eye of love,
crushed leaves casting odour
like the zeal of loneliness seeking a new heart

a flower
the colour of wallaby flesh,
a crow sounding like a man who has lost a son

fire prodded with a stick
nearly bright as the sun,
a solemn story twisted to surprise:

see the animal avoiding the line
hunters made,
taste the white flesh
wrested from fibrous ligaments the sea made,
hear the piping split sky tones
a yellow wattled bird made

touch with tender fingers
an infant only the dawn of ever returning ancient lovers
could have made.

Preminghana
Tasmania

OUT OF BOUNDS

Ineffable silence beyond the patter has an appeal. I may find the perfect poem— embodiment of silence. Beyond the glittering sun on the waves, higher than angels abandoning culture for the sake of building a new universe, I'll stay attuned to the deliverance of myopia into unobstructed sightedness.

Brushing powder in high blossoms,
rearranging them to fit the contours of my skull,
I'll open above mortally fettered growth,
odorize denuded acres
with pungency only the martyred excarnate could exude

drift limpidly
in headwinds,
expect to meet you
at the height.

You'll address me
solemnly,
declare I have no business staining pink residue
on your perfect white lips.

"Stay where you belong."

INSIGHT

If I gaze upon the first flower opening in daylight, in an absence
of influences beyond my control impinging continually on my
nerves, I could discover innocence no untoward encroachment
could sully; colorful, clear, and receptive to mild wind and delicate
rhythms, sense the flowering of my identity— witness unearthed.

Knowing no boundary
in the plenum
before I had the wit to know
I had no wit
before I penetrated the air with cries,
before I formed ears
and limbs,
through lucid blood film
bright as the moon's intangible touch
on midnight sand,
close
as the breeze ruffling hen's feathers,
still
as the reed's tips on frosty mornings

from the highest point
on a cliff,
lowest depth in the sea,
boiling water we stew our meat

I looked in my eyes.

ROYAL BLUE

If I have a limit to my vision, is it too much to ask whether the
aspiration of a smooth skinned hierophant is in my purview? Can
I rise with a disembodied soul into paradise, unfettered and secure
in the belief it will reach the being born out of the substance of air,
who will carry it into the silent color alive with light and heat, even
further into an abode that lives not for a moment but for eternity?

Turquoise lids, azure cheekbones,
blue black pupil centered in dark blue iris,
cobalt words splayed in light blue haze,
"The instant you know you have longer to live,
suffering will dissipate."

Indigo heart beating in the wind,
cerulean expanse breathing without respite,
sapphire raindrops millimeters apart,
sky blue ankles

caught

in hands reaching to touch your crown.

DESCENT

Clearly,
you would rather fondle a nape
than lick gelid sweat oozing into your eyes,
sniff the ointment soothing sun cracked skin
than odor welling from exhausted grave diggers
and open wounds

indubitably,
counting the scars on nubile limbs,
appreciate wings to hover over stolen bodies
than taste infertile egg white drying on sand

enamored with vigor,
ingest moist duck and fermented brew
than charcoal skull meat and ocular gel,
tender tips and baby's milk
than wet lime
and crackling feet

surely,
if the weight pressing you deeper
lifted a notch,
compare light above ground
with purblind admixture
with dust,
and choose the former

dilated pupils than contracting walls,
exhausted than void.

If you had your time again

would you

change?

AWARENESS

Would the Eye of Horus enable me to read a ghost's will, the
ramblings of an incubus satiated with glandular secretions, or an
Egyptian scholar's warning not to tread too heavily near a sleep-
ing cobra? Would the orb reflect rays penetrating from the solar
disc, illuminate dark insides, access the domain it decides to focus
upon, even unto the maker who brought it into being?

Stripped
of identity beyond the fullness
no one can obtain, so dense
and no cracks letting in sorrow,
I arrived light as wind,
only to find pink cloud banks,
white caps and marble turrets

languor emptied on her breast,
ardor smeared on her nipple

impotent suzerain decrying his lover's infidelity,
compelling a retinue to adhere
to truthfulness

faithful attendant creeping up behind him.

PROPHECY

In sight of a bleeding eye
the morning star will suffer
no longer in isolation,
filaments
of light instantiate behind the moon

orisons coil
from the earth's shadow,
an empyrean voice silence mortal fear

haze prolong a mountain's stillness,
droplets glow
with the surety of touching groundless ground

fall
into ephemera and gaping hearts

unto everyone, who,
disconnected
from their bloodline, alone,
will taste water

at a higher level.

GODLIKE

Distant as a candle from the sun, a sparrow from a hawk, a child from old age, how deeply we persist in our own sphere apart from the high life that condescends to taste meat on their lips. Need we be told how different they are.

Sublimating ectasis to instinct,
I'll taste pomegranate juice trickling down my throat,
hear tearing flesh, ignite ash and dust

expect inert fiber to sense my ascension,
take note
of my odour,
and stirred into the sleep of the living,
recall what I'll give

my abode—

refulgent,
incorruptible, delimited
in light constituting empires outside the aura
of the sun

I have no end.

AMONG THE IGNORANT

If insight into the void should find itself bored,
It should fall with the sun's rays
to earth

look upon a snake swallowing a vole,
substitute iron particles for indivisibility,
knowing the root
of suffering,
finding it unbearable,
limit with a cut across the eyes.

A mote under a lid should be flushed,
inflammation in tissue where light meets darkness
soothed with ointment,
incapacity to count the stars
to the very last one

douched with raindrops

even harder to count.

CALLIOPE

Whom I use for my servant
won't particularly care
if the stars, pinpoints
of perfection,
lose their brilliance,
testaments of infallibility fade into oblivion,
or the earth upheave in paroxysms
to the zenith

as long as I say
how far away black space transcends the night,
fathomless
the sea,
wide the distance between my voice
and an ear
ready to receive whatever I think essential:

green the light in a steady heart,
blue the glitter
in your eyes, red
the blood
from your veins
transfused into my skin

seen at sunset.

INDEBTEDNESS

Refreshed by the downpour,
I'll sink into the grass
and allow it to drench my backbone

enlivened by the noon day sun,
allow it to blaze on my lids and dry every vestige
of dampness

benumbed by the silence,
allow it to enter my heart
and placate the fear I'll die soon

mystified
by the pull of my body further into the dust,
slumber no more

the Muse
whom I know won't desert me
returning in the solace of resignation:

"You have rescued me from mute insensibility."

HIGH POINT

An attempt
to catch a fly with wrinkled hand
ends with failure,
the decision to raise the input
with higher thinking
ends in argument,
a calling
to translate the moon's heat
into meaning interspersed on page after page
ends with obscurity

absent my shell that smells of dust
and old age

successful.

SUNT LACRIMAE RERUM ET MORTALIA TANGUNT

(Tears form in the depths and mortality shrouds conscience)

Virgil
50 BCE

If only on a horse with flaming eyes we could tread on the clouds, with the gait of a well-bred battle charger steer even further into nebulous dust. On the outskirts of human suffering, glance backwards only once, and presume that never again, in white shawls and perfumed robes, we would be submitted to a parent's grief.

I'll carve my name on the tree
and it will bleed,
stoke the fire
and watch the flames curl around the stump,
crackling
and squeaking

water a bed of wheat
and count the spears that appear before daybreak,
nourish the shoots
and watch them instantly respond,
lifting into the blue light.

I'll grasp the tail of a lizard
and feel it part from the body,
bear the needless shock
and stand
with the wriggling piece between my fingernails

hear children after they lose footing on a cliff

screams saturating the night,
dissipating in the wind

tears mingling
in the pond where the fish swim,
and take the salt into the depths
where a bubble smothers before it rises

until,
an earthquake

and the water splashes on my forehead.

AS GREEN AS

Shall I arch into Heaven beyond their seeing
or flutter over a knife edge
with no place to land but an uplift
of air from a tainted pool,
enter the void
or descend where they bleed
and obey time, negotiate the shoals
of disillusionment

an unearthly stab in a blood red heart.

Although I barely moisten the tip
with spleen, I can see into a womb
and its need
to produce an offspring far surpassing the one
who treads on buttercups, smiles
in my light,
and enables it to grow from within

it,
though, has hands, feet
and a head

solidifying like butter on a cold day,
swirling like ink in white water,
approaching the limit of life
like a blade of grass:

scattered by a free hand,
bound in clumps,
eaten until it disappears,
and returns in a speck
no bigger than the exclamation

it is

and lives
in moisture, warmth
and light.

FLOWERING

The extent
you embedded in the soil
is the same the word embedded
in my soul,
the depth
I penetrate to find moisture
is the same a root tip pierces the substrates
compounded of droplets, granules,
and inconscient particles

unto which I would form

if I didn't have to breathe fresh air.

Glastonbury Thorn
Somerset

SELF-CONDEMNATION

If only I could be like you, so secure and certain in your vision, of the ultimate triumph of good over evil, of the pure and perfect over the salacious and cruel. But when the scales weigh my faults against my virtues, will not the rage, the bitterness, the self-interest plunge to the ground, leaving me to feel, already, the singe on my feet?

Severing the link
between the earth's riband
of scarlet
at dusk
and the blaze
of red when I hate you so,
separating the contusion under my heart
from the sky's purpureal splendor
when the sun burns at midday.

Caressing otherworldly lineaments
with outstretched fingers
while blood bubbles in a shell turned over blue flames,
exiting holes in a network of clouds
while I snake through waves
of dull grey grass.

Prophesying transparent gold,
emerald rainbows,
and seas of glass,
while inert eyes peer to the back of my skull,
losing the connection

raindrops pattering on upturned leaves

droplets that accrue, one
by one,
in the corner of my eye.

EXTERNAL AUTHORITY

In blood, lymph,
or water,
how I swim
with one arm
backwards toward the fount

in dust, grit, or sand,
wade, toes curled inward,
toward the abyss

in aether, cloud light,
sunlit air,
stream in abundant disconnect
toward the absence
of human artifice

in soil, black bone murk,
or silt,
sink with purblind eyes
toward the chimes that augur the end
of my life

in fog, swirls
of lather, or mist,
squirm restlessly in the guru blessed,
Scripture ripe,
tradition plumping,
biased righteousness

will I ever know
in which direction
I am going?

DEVOTION

I'll turn to the night sky
and contemplate the brightest object I can find

the constant,
steady glow of a solitary star,
the moon's bright demeanour,
a lonely traveller falling inexplicably
to its cessation

and surrender to the darkness.

ANOTHER TREE OF LIFE

Leaf: what shades me from the brilliance
too bright to endure,
that tears easily
if I try to climb above the height
allocated to an earthbound heart.

Twigs: the implements I'll use
to extract splinters from my skull

words that presuppose I will exist
in the same form writing now.

Trunk: a sturdy base
on which to erect the following epistle:
I am only in you,
and cannot subsist outside your love.

Roots: holding to what sustains me
even though
I can't exist
in the form given seventy years ago

no end
and no beginning,
and life in between

unheralded voice
in the darkness,
"I love you"

silence
from which it emanated and will return.

Fruit:

ability
to say what I think.

PEARL

Although my eyesight is dim,
I can make out free standing turrets
in the clouds.

Despite the fact
hearing is dulled with clamour,
I can hear an angel's approach
or,
if you will, the flutter
of wings.

My nose
may be bombarded with the stench of decay,
but odour proceeds from a flower's internal organs

one that subsists in the blue.

Unto the back of my throat I can taste rotting meat,
but I am sure, if only just perceptible,
I'll savor sweet rain

a tonic from the heights.

My heart suffocates with doubt
and confusion

the crack of bones as they land
with a fall,
an eye popping in fire,
a stab of black need to kill

but I will not relinquish the barely lit sense

ever-present,
within
and without, and now

I am loved

EMERGENCE

Cool wind is but the last vestige of visitation,
the literary genius has little else to contemplate

no fusion of ecstasy and aether,
ethereal countenance burning with love

he'll coin terms for its flight,
undulation, and whimsy

the sun scorch its zenith,
mountains receive its caress,
moonlight refresh its course toward barren lands

mimic the swirls that pick up dust
and spread to the sea

darkness swallow it whole,
the tomb stagnate its descent,
cold turn it into haze

loneliness— a teardrop hanging from a lid,
change—
empyrean fields sprouting delicate iris
to lank grass swaying in a river,
fledgling blood, and webbed feet.

Is it lucid to exhume its immanence,
rarefied though it may be

the uplift in his corpus,
visible word upon his heart?

"Selflessness reveals you
in gullet and mud

a breath of fresh air."

THREEFOLD BEING

Given a golden chariot, gilded wings or sore feet, where would I
journey? To the extreme limit of endurance, exclaiming that limit
has been reached. Polar opposites— contours of divine feet and
undulation on underwater grass, nascent life upon a spinning orb
and ductless eyes; and, immanent in flesh, figuratively, the ever-
recurring cycle of nature.

So high,
clouds provide a soft bed to slumber,
a whisper delimits sanity just below immortality:

"ice
and water's the limit of aspiration"

so deep, purple flowers meld
with blood shed from a victim's broken heart,
a worm reluctant
to delve into purblind layers beneath rocks
and shale
cuddles around a root

so ordinary, I fix my attention on the oven's centre

bread baked early morning
smelling of all that satisfies my wants

winter:
a crow poking dead limbs hanging in a grey sky,
a torch
barely visible approaching from the inclement vista

spring: mountain tops ablaze
with afternoon glow,
footsteps clattering toward the summit

summer:
wandering between Neptune and Antares,
catching sight
of rosebuds on the outskirts
of Heaven

autumn:
lone descent
into the wilderness,
blood seeping into each leaf

so far back, inertia
and movement knew one another's opposite,
called the other
"not me," and closed ranks
against annihilation

so far forward,
pursuance caught up with stillness,
abeyance
imitated volition,
impetus saturated denial with affirmation

and now,
my heart beats silently in the darkness.

ONE OF MANY

A red flower blooming in blood,
a brilliant moon stark
in a white sky, a blazing sun
in the midst of an inferno.
Where are you?

A chuckle
in laughter, a breath in the rise
and fall of loneliness
to company,
bonhomie to solitary confinement.
Are you still there?

Moisture
in a sea,
black in ebony, blue in azure.
Will you find me?

An old survivor's sutures weeping on flesh underfoot,
brawn on the battleground eaten by crows,
an ache
in the womb of pain.

If you hear this,
please give me a chance
to be identified
from the rest.

DEPENDENCE

Assume
for a moment you are the center
of the world,
the source
of nourishment for a worm to engorge its full length

you provide the force
to enable a seed to break its shell
and unfurl new life,
enliven moisture to creep up through a root
and reach fleshy outgrowth,
but have no inkling of how or why.

Would you still remain
in your darkness

hardly cognizant
of the radiant night
which sustains you?

LIBERATION

From outside the alternation
of night
and day,
not only
do we savour litheness of the exterior,
but beneath her heart,
perceivable only to the inner eye,
the essence of her calling

an empty shell cupped in brilliant hands.

Where will the purple bird fly
when brushed by lucid rays
on the first second
of her release?

So high,
unto the infertile dance on vertiginous mist,
only a speck
on a dream's extremities

or

will she find an eminent roost far below?

Through emerald wisps on black stubble,
a ghost's herbaceous pathway,
the contraction
into star speckled space and moonlit air,
with her promise
of rose scent
and white wing tips fluttering unperturbed,
touch your crown

meld
with the shadow under the eaves,
transmute bone hard encasement into brittle eggshell

fly free?

Hangzhou
China

ANNIHILATION

Steps from the blue Mediterranean,
a warrior emblazoned in light
distant from an eye within
and disembodied heads that peer,
one after the other,
at its gaze transfixed in their flow,
mindful of the Lie sublimating your need
to rise into his intensity
and never encounter its putrid gleam again,
will shrivel the mad face leering at the core.

Armenian Monastery
Jaffa

AN ABODE IN THE SOUL

The rose plucked, left to wither

the moon struck
from the night sky, forced to spiral
into ink

the stallion
haltered by an iron hand, stopped
from bolting in the fields

plumes
of white smoke suppressed by rain,
the dance of a bee pummeled by an incoming squall,
the flow of nectar impeded in hail

cold
and icicles forming under the eaves

motion toward the sun suspended,
the drive to surface on glistening petals countered,
the urgency
to locate sensitivity
in a goddess's bosom arrested.

The whippoorwill
will find voice under the floorboards,
clouds billow above frozen drains

a fallen angel,
whom we think
will never perceive the light, fettered,
dried, and warmed

before descending any further.

UNDESERVING

Gladly, on a warm day, I accompanied a young woman into the
fields and dreamt she could have been the first born of a race that
brought literature into being, the mistress of a philanderer who
excused himself from duty and exercised his acumen in market-
places across the Orient, a benefactor to an addict who needed all
the emolument tender accompaniment could give. Leaving aside
journeys swooning in self-reflection, I entered the space behind
her heart, and raising the beat into the present, eschewed what she
could have been in unaccompanied flights, if she hadn't in a mo-
ment of susceptibility surrendered unto an unintelligible advance.

My love drew circles on my forehead
and through each
I could see clouds encompassing soft grass,
a stream tumbling over rocks,
lips about to kiss

buoyant and head up over cataracts,
alive with froth,
nubile limbs awaiting their turn

white
lilies growing in abundance

bruised easily, forsaken
by herbivores,
spreading at will
from one plot to another,

not once dug up
and fed to the pigs
or left to wilt as noon heat grows

back through the gel,
outwardly perceptive,
blue flecked iris, unruffled hair

she
who forsook the bravest and noblest

to lie alongside me.

CONSECRATION

A witness to the cosmos:

luster born of surrender
on its way back to Heaven,
a flight to the stars

an earthbound ray stunning the nonchalant
into submission,
internment in the darkness

wasteland into enrichment,
poverty
into plenty,
silence into the host's acclamation:

embody the black mark
and destroy it
in the inferno,
my zeal

light washed heavenly spirit,
the flow through my veins

the brazen, burnished rod,
my spine

the injured, but insightful organ,
my eye

the steadfast limb,
my leg

the never-ending love

Yours.

Crusader Church
Ramla

BARELY VISIBLE

In order to truly escape the confines imposed from birth, I need
the wings of a mythical bird like a Persian simurgh or Chinese
roc, and to translate cold feet into air, tired hands into an updraft,
a wilting spine into freedom to fly anywhere, unbeholden to the
force that pulls us ever toward the earth.

Before I drop back
in a squall to crevices
and white stained outcrops,
emptying my head of the tang of salt,
I would like to rinse my feathers
in cloud light,
douche my organs in silver moon rays

eminently soaring in tenderest blue,
lathe
my eyes
in the fine spray emptying from the Overseer's heart.

ICTHUS

Take me
to the bottom
where I'll linger at the source:

the moon turned liquid,
stars dripping white essence willy nilly.

Chancing my luck against a boiling sun,
carry me to the surface
where I'll take a breath,
and you'll drink me with cupped fingers.

Finding my way through rusting ironwork,
a cracked ceiling
and dirty beams,
flood a simple heart into the sea

fishes swimming side
by side
with tensile backbones that can avoid a hook.

Chalice Well
Glastonbury

COLD COMFORT

Ghosts flutter on the skyline,
lips shriek of corpses laid out on silt,
the vagabond weeps before the impenetrable cliff

I will lift my veil
and peer at them one by one.

The flood rises above the eyeline,
bulbous features sink below the waves,
grass sways on the floor

I'll leave a dry space on my palm.

Breath tastes
of rotten cabbage, tongues twirl
in pus

I'll swallow the golden glow saturated in dew.

Wounds ooze noisome fumes,
organs give off malodor
when crushed

I'll search the rose for fragrant shadows.

Molten drips burn through the fabric separating you
from that dead end, that isolation,
that mangled sense
of senselessness

I will hold you
in my arms
and shed a tear on your forehead.

NARCISSUS

At the instant you fly
from ethereal time,
what will you see?

Flecks
of ash,
an eye peering unobstructed on a forehead

children holding up a leg found by the wayside,
the center
where love is stoked

a razed village, voluminous interior
pregnant
with repose

lips that celebrate the newborn
in the charnel
at the end of the lane,
the word ushered in the cruel expanse
you would prefer not to see

or your own reflection?

FOR ITS OWN SAKE

A few people
by now
have given up looking into the center
of the blossom

pink reminds them
of hands after washing clothes,
tinge of brown
fading to the edges— the end

folds
in petal's growth— ageing
under their chins,
softness—
bed

aroma—
a newborn sprinkled
with talc,
powder—
dust upon a tomb

and I, a little longer

for I forget such things.

ON THE BOTTOM RUNG

The vein from my heart

a conduit of light
and love?

No. I am too niggardly
in my ways.

My mouth, an opening for sweet words
of wisdom?

No. I am too caught up
in wondering what my next meal will taste like.

My feet planted
while my hands reach to Heaven in gratitude.

No. I am still grinding out the same track
on my way
to meet a pal
with whom to share my latest joke.

Yet, in moments of solitude,
I'll still blacken my vision,
arrest the images from entering
and face,
if that be the word,
the nescience.

For the moment you think you may not be,
you are.

For the moment
you assume you are intoxicated
with reality,
you are not.

In the time it takes to think you're in the presence
of the almighty divine,
you are merely sensing your own joy
in being alive.

MORTAL SIN

I've grown used to fine wines,
cutlets stewed in spice
and herbs,
and the tenderest loin on plates carved from ivory

you,
however, subsist on leeks
and water.

I have plunged deeply into folds
of nakedness, inhaled the scent
of sweat mingled with frankincense,
caressed under parts with a lingering finger

you persist with a solitary gaze
on white clouds and insect trails.

My bed is softer
than feathers drawn from a goose's midriff,
my toilet inlaid with porphyry

you repose on a worm addled log
and pee
where the trees grow alongside the graveyard.

I could ascend
to ever-growing petunias

you, after a long and arduous abnegation
of rosewood handles and myrrh–

accoutrements to the grave–

crawl to the isolated peak you call home.

I'll carve my name
on my accomplishments:

the erudite text witnessing the foibles
of human character, streets swept clean
on ordering menials to their tasks

you, however, disappear into detachment,
a surfeit
of loneliness and light filled blood.

I envy you.

TRUE TO ONESELF

A grain
of sand upon the wound
that is my silence,
a fleck of soot
on the eye
that is the gateway for your entry,
a milliliter of sweat
on the skin
that could reflect the eternal glow.

It might as well
be a boulder,
a weight exceeding a ton,
a lashing of burnt cream.

For the instant
I disregard the stain,
a rent appears

in the moment
I apperceive Heaven,
Hell invites its own upheaval.

A man.

MADONNA ACROSS THE STREET

Ah, vital light, soft rays of blessedness,
Languidly dust motes drift to my finger,
Frankincense swirls nearly fade and linger.
In recompense for the imbroglio of distress–
Green almond juice bitter in full ingress–
Candle lit interior, melodious bell ringer,
Vitreous luminance, co-sanguineous harbinger—
Plenipotential womb, veridical witness.

Brazen chalice lifted to burning lips,
Man handled crust savored upon my tongue,
Sacrosanct fields aflame with tender tips,
Immortal growth reaching the bottom rung.
But, oh, the moist contours of her red lips,
Palatable nectar of *her* blithe tongue.

FORTY YEARS ON

Where once was wine,
mead,
and juice crushed from an apple,
now
only the trickle from an icicle

where you heard whistles,
flutes,
and drums rolling out paeans,
the voice parched in need
of an angelic whisper trembling in the sockets

where the witness to immortal fields glowed–
resignation of matter to holy appurtenance–
only bare boards, stone, and white walls.

The warm shudder before sleep
and eyes that see further
than an eagle
in flight

hardly,
chilblains and blurred edges

scent in high altitudes

the must
of an unwashed cape,
long overdue sponging under your breast

the approach
of love conforming with the lift in your heart

no,
inflammation
and gauze on open skin

the dance
on a turning wheel flowering into abundance

in the six-foot square retreat,
only a crouch and aching back.

THEATER

Return, ghost,
and let me know what it is like
where you dwell,
for I may find myself where you are
one day.
Placate
my fear, oh apparition,
the suffering is not as bad as we have it
in the hovels under the bridge.
Sing, blessed chorus

intimate the next world free of rotten carcasses,
flowing blood
and blindness.

When the curtains are drawn,
I want to gaze on flowers larger than my head,
swim
without restriction through mist oceans,
reel with the shriek
in my doleful ears

it is better
to avoid cold wavering between two worlds.

My vision
will be of the lucent creature translating vista
of abode
into gesture:

the surprising rapidity rain tumbles—
elbows stiff
then loose,
the morgue dissipating in sunlight—
eyes penetrating to the aura behind my skull,
cleanliness
of the air—
the morning draught deep as the feet.

I will watch mildew grow on a discarded blade,
the moon glide
over placid water

salt cheeked,
float beyond grey innards sucking half-light

the simple inference:

the gleam in an eye— starlight,
a raised lid—
the wish
to travel, black shadow—
the stretch to distant shores

a sonorous tone—
an elemental force called upon
to reside in my breast,
speak
of a breeze that isolates pollen
on a mountain bloom,
spreads plum scent through a crowded village

leaves dead leaves in the gutter.

UNATTACHED

If you are truly free, you could end up anywhere. There is no prece-
dent, past life, or divine will to order an outcome. The moon could
fling from orbit, the sun descend until it melts your brain, and
clinging to a vine curling upwards end up in grime. Or you may
find the stars cleansing your forehead of sweat, the beating heart
beating a rhythm in the belly of Jupiter, and a ghost, transcendent
to its demise, reappearing to the eye it once belonged, retracting
from the blue aura, descrying the apparition it thinks you are.

Drying your eyes in the heat from her womb,
implanting the will to perceive in each socket,
excising the shadows swirling in abundance,
could you lift from the egregious tomb,
penetrate topsoil weighing upon the rivulet
barely trickling, hardly alive—invariance

until, secretly, unasked for, lovingly,
harboring no need for repayment,
she'll flow with your tears, shine in your darkness—
purblind, maybe incumbent in mystery,
the full extent of her involvement,
still, out of immanence, witness

blue folds enveloping the curve of her motherhood,
the barely expectant nod toward imminent arrival,
ever present aura encircling her stature—if only
graced with the scent of a thigh smeared with blood,
a short, sharp cry, almost irreverent call—
hear an answer, succinctly, verily

with prescient gifts allocated to flesh and bone,
immaculate breath following pursuers of the righteous,
why you succumbed to the crushing wheel,
encountered the grave, a monotonous tone
amplifying space from which you'll leave:
"It is freedom that you feel."

AN ELEMENTAL'S ODE

Envelop me
with light
and I'll taste scorching odor,
smell its eager consumption,
face lemon scented brightness.

Free me to dance on the wind,
paint transparent arcs on a firefly's course
and, lithe as a cat chasing string,
reach the wandering planets
and frolic
in the sun's updraft of heat.

Entrust me to the fallen earth
and I'll flow with slurry,
settle in grey clay,
balance
on my hands upended
in rubble after a landslide.

Let me swim
in croaking pools
and I'll sing
of rainbow dust, golden wave lengths,
and the martyr expecting rewards
for drowning in river floods
left unattended
to the very end.

Hold me under, with the full weight
of lymph and blood,
and I'll surface

in springs

circling his heart.

INVISIBLE FRIEND

Steep in a cloud's moisture
and let droplets form under your lids,
near
to the tearful vizier of millennia beforehand
who only sought coarse matter
that formed his fingers
and resin that held him firmly together,
enamored
with blood dripping from extended joints,
carved flesh and bleating

yet
at daybreak the water welled,
quenching his thirst

jagged impulses suffocating in serenity,
silver threads and silence entwining need to speak:

"One much greater
than I will ever be."

Walk
on hard rock
and feel the flint under your feet,
the same as when the traveler cut his tendons
on sacred ground

white minarets barely visible though the haze.

Refuse to string pearls around a waist
and gaze longingly
into a cleavage lathed in sweat,
near enough to a scholar who eschewed rich meat
and goat's milk flavored with spices

sunset reddening swollen dates and fronds.

In the manner of an unknown witness,
who timed his pulse
with the lapping of the tide
into an inlet,
the murmur of his breast
with the lifting of a veil
on a beauty's first night,
and the tingling in his nerve endings
with the aromatic fall
and surge of expectation,
repose
in the sweet meat auguring the taste
of longevity

a pupil to an iris, an iris in light.

Indent the sand
with your forehead,
and leave an imprint resisting the burning wind

in the wake of mystical love–

the nail hard sheen drawn from the blue sea,
the vast unexplored stretching beyond eyesight–

as if
you've no desire to die,
sit in the heat congealing in the shadows,
embrace the cool wind floating across the waves

lonely no more.

Abu Dhabi
Arabian Peninsula

A POET IN OUR MIDST

The rose glow
bade me to look unencumbered
into the first light entering from the deity
no one else could embody,
an even more lustrous web hanging above the clouds
enticed me to swivel my neck as far back
as the horizon to my rear

I should have minded my footsteps
on the path to the altar.

Cobblestones unevenly spaced, a toe easily trapped

headlong onto my face.

Luckily, perchance,
Ambrose walking by lifted me to my feet

the ice pack
on my head numbing the bruise,
the gauze on my eye stemming the flow, the drips
from my vein staunched by a loving finger.

"Stargazing again,
Euphemius, searching beyond the night
for efflorescence burning a door
for you to enter and hide away.

Enamored
with sojourns transcendent beyond faith,
remaining ensconced
in beatitude known only to your illuminated cells:

purveyor
of sustenance to the lonely planets,
echo
of dying multitudes hidden in the darkest abyss,
the word of the forlorn lying comatose in a ditch
between perpetual absence and interminable nothing.

Here,
drink this soup prepared with piquant herbs
and vegetables raised in our garden

the flowers are in full bloom.

Rest your head
on my shoulder,
let your weight sink into my bones

never mind your blood staining my robe.

Tell me again
of how high you fly.

I like to repeat your visions,
if only
for the briefest period

it makes me feel that I am free."

SABI

Old man stretching paper on a frame
under cherry blossoms—
one finger missing.

An actor's solemn mask drooping below hairline—
feet missing a step.

Seagull's circling a dead fish—
guts splayed in moonlight.

An eye
nowhere near the smattering
of details—

closed against bitter wind.

SEQUENCE OF LATER HEAVEN

Green shoots, tall reeds—
and the thunder rolls

rising wind,
white fluff caught on the tips—
and bodies huddle
one to one

newborn lids, purblind—
and the sun breaks through

naked folds,
pink underlip—
and
milk wells on a nipple

saturated mouth, quieted nerves—
and a head nuzzles further

a scar
across her back, a gouge
in her rump—
and she tastes malignant air

a trickle
of saliva,
exposed teeth—
and he stalks the perimeter

a shift in the wind,
a nest well hidden—

and they settle into sleep.

I Ching: King wen's arrangement of the trigrams

EVANESCENCE

I can't
say what you are,
where
you abide,
or whether
your true qualities
persist over millennia

and I say
'you'
because the instant
of visitation is so intimate,
personal and sweet,
it could only be another
like a mother
who fondled my hair,
a father who touched my brow
through pain

it was,
it went

and for all the world
I want it to return—

the lift in my heart.

FAIRY TALE

A frost-tinged eyelash between a cross
on the outskirts of satanic devourment
and fingers curled
in submission to the god
of shamelessness,
Cruelty
toward a whimpering kitten
and fondling dead nakedness
in an orbit around a thigh.
A chorus far away as Saturn
and the pallor drowning a blemished moon.

Allow the blood to flood a cold eye
and well into tears that splash the arches
of your feet, squint
in the glow suffusing the gelid landscape
and infer the shape
of flesh lacerated
between lilium white spreading through light
and, straggling through the undergrowth,
an open snowdrop

fill it
with beauty reminiscent
of a bloom on an angel's cheek.

OBEISANCE

Everyone
can be provident, lucid,
and beatified
in the space no animal will tear,
dragon rip out sinews,
or gainsay the ever-present beat

calm now as the waves subside.

Could Zeus be the progenitor?
An Arabian night rider?
Poseidon's offspring?
Venerable psalms surfacing in an immaculate throat?

I am one
with humanity,
I presume no ground outside of dedication
to the one true faith:

all proceed from the same center
and return to the one source

the force of idolatry
abeyant in the lift to perceive elucidation
in an iris,
insignificant in the speck that evaporates time.

I submit
to the cause:

oneness, heartedness

the world's cavernous yawn before sleep.

Bahai Gardens
Haifa, Israel

USELESSNESS

Indebted to Santoka Taneda 1882–1940 whose poems can be discerned— translations, more or less, of the originals.

Resting until the moon reaches slumber.

If you lay right in the middle of its pronouncement on earth, you may dream of its candor that will glow until you can see what motivates you to be so dissolute, what inspires you to write, what motivates you to walk endlessly.

Autumn wind, forever walking, walking.

What have you achieved? What good have you accomplished? The autumn wind may know—its chill, its presumption of cold to come may provide a clue: footsteps crunching a long trail, the way disappearing in ice, restlessness ending in the darkest hue.

Unto the end, tramping over dry grass.

Just like it you it decreases, just like you it dissolves. Smells like raw skin needing to freshen up, and not likely to live beyond the morrow.

Neither alive nor dead, a persistent wind.

When you wander, the wind frames your warmth with a chill. Lonely yes, despairing no. Solemn yes, helpless no. Unable to tell from where it comes, pushing you toward an unknown destination.

Alone, a mountain— beyond once more, a mountain.

A rueful smile, overcoming an obstacle, and another rising up before you. And you know there will be another— puddles and pools, gorges and crevices, the rift in your spleen, the bruise on your liver.

Further, deeper— deeper, further— green mountains.

And you walk as I would do, only again and again into the heart and through the night of the limbs.

Reluctance to turn one's head, hurrying down the road.

There is no ephemerality worthy of sustaining, no future worthy of finding out what will happen. There is the now, and it has already passed.

Unaware of the moon's fall into deep darkness.

What must you do? Prepare your bed where you stand? A few leaves for a pillow, a branch for a blanket, the soothing quality of night a coverlet for your tired aching feet?

Opening, facing this way— fragrant white flowers.

They turned to you to render their secrecy, purity, selflessness— receptive to all that is good in the universe.

In the shade of a rock water sure to be bubbling up.

Do you see it, or do you just hope for it? Have you a diviner's sense, or just make believe you have the capacity to delve into the nature of things? But you know, and can already taste, in anticipation, the sweet water on your lips.

Living alone, bright green, fresh grass.

You have time to look earnestly, efface your looking; wave a pointed tip, scrawl out fresh lines ; hear color bleeding toward the sun.

RE-ENTRY

On the outskirts of mortality, I could meet a fellow traveler who'll
tell me he has gone further than I could ever have done, his envi-
rons are not suitable for a heart that wants to stay perpetually im-
mersed in brightness ascending even further or exults in a sojourn
away from the exigencies below.

Each whorl
on each thumb, print
on each finger,
indentation
on each foot lifted from the surface
into thin air

every speck
in every eye, mote
on every iris, color
under every lid went dark
instantaneously
as you ascended into the stratosphere,
and retained its original place

only lighter

when you plunged into the earth.

STRANDED ON THE CONFLUENCE OF THE STYX AND THE RHINE

This poem is a response to the Paul Celan poem, 'The Straightening'

Visionaries aspire to the cynosure—

scented phlox
on timorous winds,
reconstituted star cluster, immortal gaze
at light

follow a renewed entity expanding to distant pinpricks
in Heaven—

open pulse, inert blaze on the periphery
of sanity, gateless entrance

reach the edges
of Babel's fractured palate—

angelic impedance,
seraphic sword, empty zone

drop into warm milk stained with midnight—

the pogrom's slow march
into silence,
genuflection
with no fingers, tympani with no beat

find the heretofore undiscovered voice
between the children caught in a storm
and white blotter cancelling every echo mooted from far flung
    dynasties.

A–

men.

NOW AND AGAIN

If the radiant aura around her skull
were ever present,
most probably
I would worship her
as I would a deity.

If the haze lingering over ripe green grass
were to prolong visitation,
I would scoop it
and lathe my face and eyes.

If the lucid touch
upon a rose
were to persist through noon until evening,
I would sink into the glow
until slumber caressed the vertex denuded of black spot,
rust, and infoliated eyes.

If the world I knew surrendered to dulcet tones
readily congruent
with the light of their issuance,
I would rise on its breath
and feel the heat of wayward moons beneath my feet

but only for an instant.

IRRESPONSIBILITY

Although a compassionate lover may never caress my neck
unless I survey the eyes
of a pauper or the sores
of a child locked in deformity,
I'll concentrate solely on the rise to lapis lazuli—
the facade of ziggurats striving toward the sun

the surreal black night,
inebriated songsters pining for the entrance
to the tunnel which precedes their demise,
celestial candles showing the pathway

yet, if only divulging the ectasis resounding in light,
the propinquity
of eyes that shine inwards outward,
can I say that uselessness doesn't saturate every clause
and the reader will chance upon their vacuity

with the thrust of a nib into stained paper,
leave a mark in the years
to come

the outpouring of one who provides an alternative
to fishing for coins
in a muddy stream.

ANGEL ON THE LOOSE

I can hardly tell
whether the ant that crossed my path
was in search of food
or returning to a nest
with a morsel to distribute amongst its brethren,
but I do know
it scurried as fast as it could.

I am unsure
whether the rain swelling the creek outside my door
will come again
with same intensity,
but I know the smudge in the sky turning darker
is encroaching over the rooftops.

I cannot perceive
if your heart beat quicker
when the thunder crashed intensely last night,
but I do know
mine did

and
sooner or later
it will again when I see you pass my door.

LOVE INCARNATE

At the end of the tunnel—
an illuminated tree
and a bright land far removed
from the rabid stare
and clamor.

Here—
burnt to cinders lungs inhaling plastic fumes.

There—
morning song,
night trust burning like a star
in abeyance of heat.

Here— swamps exuding toxic odor
colored green.

There— nonchalant,
replete,
creating substantial rest,
becoming enamored with all that moves.

Why bother to come here,
returning reluctantly
into a sack of blood,
bone and skin stretched to its limit?

On the off chance,

on a good day,

you can smile to a neighbor.

HIGHER THAN HELL

Where are you
when swathes
of long grey grass wave backward
and forward
as if in an underground current,
disembodied heads float up
and blank eyes stare into your own?

In the breast of an unknown ruminant
who descended
to observe dead matter becoming conscious
of lifelessness?

In the maw
of a bloodless fish
who swims with no purpose
up and down the Styx?

In the eye of a forgotten well
where the bucket balanced on mud
barely lifts into the dream

douched

with spring water?

IF I WERE NOUS

The same as I would carve my initials
on a trunk,
I'd leave my name on your diaphragm

build a wooden hut
to keep out the winds and rain,
implant firmly a place of repose
in your sternum,
resist the invective
and curses which assail the vulnerable

splice string with hard twill
to make it stronger, entwine my backbone
with yours
so we would say we were one.

You are in the mortal's cage
of woe,
the heart beating musically
in abnegation of tomorrow forever,
a coda lasting long as a whiff
of silence on aether

you could,
in tracing the nomenclature that I am
in the plenitude of night, last a little longer.

ALMOST IN THE FOOTSTEPS OF BASHO

There is no need to visit sacred landmarks
and rub my fingers into the groove
a traveler felt led closer to the one
who, first, breathed on the stone

the moist ground
where an eye begets images of fire
and mountain rising on an ascending trail,
earth and sun setting on furze,
is enough to stay put.

It isn't necessary
to follow the stars
as if to a brighter confluence on the far side,
or tread on the same path an ancient explored
in order to refresh the dust

in the absence
of a settled abode,
likening the drifting clouds to a mystical home,
the black wilderness before my eyes
to eternal solitude that precedes all light,
afternoon rain
to teardrops congealing in wide open space.

Until the morning sun rises in marrow,
lighting strikes bland tissue,
and water pours from uninhabited glades

all I must do

is journey within.

THE DISTANT JOY OF LIGHT

When the waves break on the shore,
wind blows off the cliff,
and spray drenches the rock I was standing on
only a minute before,
descrying the missive inscribed by an emperor
who, immanent in the pulse,
could distill lymph in skin bags
when the moon shudders while descending,
is dependent
on the imprint on pith
and the air around each word that surfaces underfoot:

"With sacred potion lathering my eyes,
I'll see into the inferno, grow beyond earth's mortal shell
and the never ending splash
on my feet

wash my brain,
corral the stars in my heart,
languish in serenity
where disquieted eyes peer from a distance

nectar
in a snowdrop filling the air around a swimming head

and the surf,
rising and reaching the epicenter
of bliss, will,
with little effort, sweep me into the undertow

sinking, and tasting the foam beneath my feet,
scrawling blindly:

scarlet fish chew upon the thread combining utterance
with red anemones in bloom,
dissolve toward ink lit up by midnight

orifices clam shut,
sputum curdles every healthy node,
rose welters
like plague on the skin

umbilical dregs
red,
ripe, and juicy bruise little bones

subzero baby's eyes see the spear sticking her womb.

I'll drink from gushing veins if I'm free to go.

Mother's blood? Too raw to face the nemesis
who'd risk defilement
to color her milk, spike a beating heart
to taste its pulse,
fire the soothsayer's daughter
to raise a light

in the grace of that glow,
look at the flickering on her final words:

'Moisture on a frail leaf, sweat on a heart

the seagull's flight above the headland,
a bubble floating on the moon's aura

bright blue swell
and white froth, spittle and heaven gone eyes

red raw sunset, drowning in vital fluid

your craving to leave the body.'"

OUT OF REACH

I shall approach the stars as if every light were mine
to show up airborne scintilla crafted in their likeness

illumination revealing debris swept out of sight,
a plane transmogrified from absence
of night

the way of hierarchies
where only blossom odour
is palatable

an eventual, unsurpassed notion.

"Undivided as early winter's frost on high boughs,
we subsist on shadows entwining flight
and luminance beyond mortal realms

spiraling so far
we have no contact with friend,
sibling,
or lover

to the heights without a word
of consideration that reaches a neglected soul
embodied deep as a rainbow underground."

BALANCE

Can silk undulate on cosmic breath
and calm an upturned forehead?
Am I wanted?
Have I caressed new limbs interlacing clouds
in the blue? Is this my task?

In what manner did I strive—

wet lipped
into the night,
relishing the haste to unveil holy ineffability

alert,
on the lookout for rifts in the brain,
allowing in globules lately condensed
from holy mother's skin?

Do I really want to cavort
with the disembodied, fly through empty cities
until the extreme smells like burnt dust
and miniature landscapes drop away?

Should I remain
where ice forms puddles
and drips into eyes blinded by snow light,
forget
to spread ointment on galaxies and,
where the shadow meets the bird's broken wing,
make a cast out of dust and paste

anticipate the journey is up and down

without neglecting one or the other

and losing both?

JOURNEY

At midnight,
ice cracks
and a gust from the river extinguishes the lantern.

Please say something to dispel the gloom—

momentum
from the heart between subliminal night
and the expanse that throws up chatter and profanity.

"Reclusive
as the ancient poet,
who sought mystical truisms in the luminous age
when the divine word melded with every utterance,
believe, when eyelids close
and the substance
fine as afternoon sunlight settles under your breath,
you can establish rapport.

'Unbeknownst to the emperor,
who prayed for the return
of a mandate to keep order
when the suffering
in his provinces became too much to bear,
a bulb broke through frost and unfurled

even though his queen couldn't love the suitor
who embodied her heartbeat,
the moon was alive with fragrance
and dust glittered in the light.

Whatever is,
there is something else

whatever will be,
there will be another.

You mustn't overwhelm nonchalance
with ardor,
nor sorrow with joy

nor can you take a blossom and eradicate winter.

Whatever blooms will fade,
whatever fades will bloom.

Either or, you are within it
and out of it.

Aware that no one else had passed by
in the landscape denuded of any feature
that could reveal her whereabouts,
a solitary figure,
dark against snow driven air,
expected a companion approaching from the opposite direction.

Hours now.

Communion imminent.

'The moon is barely visible,
but we'll make our way
on the road that appears through the drifts.

Listen to the roar
as if its force was vying to enter an aperture in your head.

Abide for a while in the fissures
between the boulders where the air is still.

Witness the source that could motivate you:

a disrobed monk swimming offshore for a mile
before he sinks,
a lover who demands you bleed into his wounds,
the wraith
who manages to interpose between a word
or two of kindness,
swallowing them whole

sunlight on the waves three fathoms deep,
an empty shoreline, olive trees pressing against the hill,
smoke trickling from numerous chimneys,
a blazing blue sky devoid of any cloud

a contrite wayfarer
on the move from an empty vale to an arbour
in the garden full of sap and well-tended,
from glutinous night to light sprinkling mistletoe twigs
heightened for a kiss.

'I am not yours to call your own.
I do not belong to you,
nor do you possess anything other than nothing

and that isn't yours.'"""

VOCATION

Intoxicated
with the blue fly oozing drowsiness above his brow,
a white robed savant sprawled under a gingko tree:

With your wings
the planetary bodies would not be beyond my reach

with your eyes I could perceive a safe place
to land,
with one nerve engulf my brain
with cloud drift spun into a ball
of white

empty my heart of charm,
replace it with a simple desire
to lay my eggs
in the rotting carcass beneath me.

POET FOREVER

Weeping blood and shivering like a fox
in a green nest,
it could be one of the ghosts that tormented Li He

retarding growth in the liver, a bibulous swine

in the throes,
floating like jetsam on a black, underground river,
a disembodied head dissuading me
from teasing open each blossom,
tasting lime on high boughs,
and allowing the scent to permeate grey mist
on its flow

yet, through valleys, defiles
and to the heights,
light glistening on the leaves,
I must treasure my brief sojourn
and empty my heart

a vein bursting in what I see:

a skull cradled
by its mother,
fields strewn with corpses,
an ancestor holding a torch before his men:

"You
will vanquish the enemy,
open the barricades,
illumine glittering eyes."

An ancient composing notes on the bones
at his feet.

"I have no other
whom I would want for the meeting
of two lives,
of two minds, of two hearts.
I have no desire
to be elsewhere

only with you, only by you

will you reconfigure my every utterance?

"A light wind from the wasteland
brings an odor of burnt dust
and ageing flesh."

(I can but listen on the outskirts.)

"A spot of rain
and dark, thick clouds loom on the horizon.

Nightshade will always take root,
future seeds sprout

one most high,
far ahead as the dying sun,
will listen to you."

LONG-TERM AFFILIATION

Perhaps,
in another millennium
you'll relinquish the permanent and inviolate entity
sufficient unto self-fulfillment,
enter the heart regenerating the decayed,
the stricken,
the captive who cringes at the baying hound
in the distance

take time,
too, to look back at your shadow

when rain comes on the wind,
and every detail's made clearer,
speak of fine veins on a lid
and rosebuds under the awning,
drink tea
and settle your differences

a beginning
which has no end,
a deep which clings to the surface

love which is yours,
as the heartbeat is hers
to fold into love

ensure
you give the food that touches nerves,
and conjoins yesteryear
with the potency of the present,
giving as you have been given—

a spray of white blossom,
hands the colour of powder,
a mother's diary

words of tenderness soft as a kiss:

"You need not be reluctant,
everyone can enjoy the source—

the fount engendering songs
with an ancient lilt
and, perchance,
your own warble like a nightbird":

You will change me,
turn me into a seeker,
lead me
where I haven't been,
inspire me out of confinement

touch my lips,
and while the Spring is in flower,
the gate open
and wind suppressing clamour,
I'll sing along with you:

My words are the dew,
the dawn
is my word

my words within the sleeping breast,
within the morning mist rising from the coast.

THIRD MILLENIUM CE

In unfamiliar garb reminiscent of purpureal clouds,
retreating from inebriation
and a penchant for guzzling noisome fluid,
I'll drench my ligaments
in dew
and wait for noon to evaporate me into strata
near to drones burnt out from a heady chase,
naiads inscribing goodwill messages
on earth's canvas,
a sorcerer's implant in unborn tissue
materializing an infant who can light fire in retina,
illuminate a golden iris
and, at the end of her fingertips,
touch the morning star
as it aligns with her sister
in space
no one has discovered

branches clustered heavily with fruit,
rainbow blue lighter than air,
one white cloud

as far as possible
from oil tasted on the back of my throat.

FOREVER AND ANON

I can observe a grain of sand,
apportion a word
to the beat
of wings of a butterfly
or to the pulse in a vein flowing toward the heart.

I can observe the small
and the large and the light
and the heavy, as equally
as I can contemplate the rise
of breath into air
on a frozen morning,
the scent through clouds and snow
to a mound of earth beneath

a transparent shadow letting out the twinkle
in both eyes
and obscuring the foment of affliction

spread through each ear,
a permeable veil letting through ingress
coeval
with purity
and holding no defence
against echoes from dying epochs

the outside looking inwards surpassing the outside.

The first time
I saw you folding paper into the shape
of a heart,
heavenly orbs translated into vowels
and the very silence preceding life itself
into a hush afore announcement:

"Everywhere
I see you,
alive,
waiting.
Each time
I see you, my heart sings its song:

You are all I want,
all I care for.

You are my delight,
my path's rest,
my beloved."

OMEGA

You could be the divine Son who breathes life into every bud, the extraordinary messenger who delivers in the throes of fear, in warmth out there, the positive declaration of accompaniment. So, too, it could be, when the light is dimming and the scratch against the window could be a spider, a twig, or an insect flying to its end, the one in a lifetime, "I am."

At the day's end we walked along the shoreline
and threw pebbles into the froth

the bubbles increasing until they reached the rocks
and popped, one
by one, releasing salt air
into the odor
of ice and wind from the polar regions.

If God feels the heat of your need,
why let an unknown entity crush the spring
in your heart
and sup on tender shoots?

Softened by moonlight
we listened to the wind in the pines.

Without ardor,
space will be found in which our world would collapse.

After midnight we surrendered unto the incoming tide
and allowed it to sweep into our breasts.

Inside the bounds inhabited by the makers
of solace,
I'll swallow the night that could swallow me whole,
counter affliction,
and nurture the flower blossoming in the centre.

A chorus floating on ghostly pallor:

"Confine her
in a mixture of gluttony and sloth,
mold our lips to brush naked limbs,
strike pearl white teeth with flint."

I'll nurture a rose in sediment
that will grow beyond the dew,
mirroring it
in its entirety.

"Smother her veins,
scrape her sensitive skin."

I'll place an ode perfectly on every misbegotten utterance
and watch it dissolve,
as if it could never arise again

neutral and impotent
by the magic of transformative abundance
that,
with the vast night filled waters giving up to a black ocean,
I'll illuminate the distance between sensitivity concocted of nectar,
spice, and morning light,
and a mordant bruise

for the glow will intoxicate my spine,
the scent inveigle my thoughts,
leading me to suspect
I am a Saviour,
a god averring the capacity
of an entranced minion
to capture the innate qualities of the transcendent,
a solitary poet eliminating the source of suffering.

But
I suspect this to be absurd.

In the annals of a forgotten future,
at the root of matter a seed will grow
into tendrils reaching sublime air

yellow light and yellow bloom,
pink tinged petal
and pink countenance looking down on us

dew sliding down the outgrowth
into our hearts.

I am only through You.
I am certain solely in Your being.
I have no value
without your love.
I am only in You.

A YEAR SLOWLY TURNING

A response to Rudolf Steiner, the Twelve Virtues

Early Spring

AT YOUR DISCRETION

You'll brush cobwebs from my suit
and rearrange the flower
on my lapel—

no one
should be left to die unattended and neglected.

I'll present my corpse
to Heaven
and, maybe, with a fresh look
from eyes that look into the deeds
that prolonged my stale odor,
I'll be given another chance.

Mid Spring

2 AM

Even though she can't see them,
I'll place the camelia blossoms on her table—
red as the rims around my eyes.
After soup,
barely sipped,
I'll read her favorite poem—
doggerel at best.
When the lights go out,
and visitors are meant to leave,
I'll still sit by her side
and pretend
no one will see me—

quiet
as her long,
drawn out breath

as the curtain is pulled aside,
say:

"Just for one more moment,
please."

ON THE SAME PLANE

The morning sun will glaze my forehead,
just as the sunset will leave its red welcome
on my neck

my heart will crave your smile,
just as my thought wants to deliver a reason why
the clouds are so white

the blossom will open, just as surely
as the bee will close its wings
when it settles into pollen and nectar

and, when a breath
of fresh air, silent as midnight,
rests on my palm.
I will acclaim the light filled spirit entering buds
and swirling the stalks.

ONWARD AND UPWARD

When a green persimmon drops on my roof,
I'll ignore the clatter
and add another three hundred words
to the book
I have been writing for thirty years.

The pages are yellow, stale,
and oddly curved,
something like the heart that's been at it
since the first drop of ink splattered

in remembrance
of a word descending from outer space.

Mid Summer

ANTICIPATION

When I speak
of bamboo,
its sharp, pointed leaves, bright green
in the sun,
tough stalks raising constantly into the blue,
am I talking about bamboo
or profusion
and will
to proliferate over other plant life?

When I contemplate the earth
full of rotting leaves,
and dark
only as it can assume,
am I talking about the soil
or disposition to retreat into the night?

When I think
of one, unbroken cloud
enhanced with distance from Pluto's cold heart,
am I considering immanent rest,
lack of impetus

or, if only for a moment,
cessation of volition

before I meet another term?

COMPLETION

When the bird had been crushed
by a wheel, it lay eyes wide open,
flapping one tiny wing.

So, as to relieve solitary agony
I held it under water in a bucket.

The heart still beat furiously—

all determination
to persist
as if the universe was trying to strive through fiber
and rise into the heights
not easily quelled.

But
it was soon enough

and the beat entering through my fingers
and into my heart

stopped.

POLITENESS

I have no answer for the salvo of insults.
"You really do nothing all day,
selfishly keeping your nose above white paper
and scribbling a few lines?
Have you anything important to say."

Well,
if the truth be known, you may be right.
I do sense an aura of redundancy,
a cloud of uselessness hovering over my hand.

Would you like a cup of tea?

TWILIGHT

I'll dress in shades of brown, tan,
and ocher

with a snow white shirt and black tie,
visit the chapel sited under yellow leaves
and grey branches

with deep solemnity, seek to borrow a hint
of blue courage to face the ordeal I must face
when my time comes

it is only a matter of months now,
so they said in the infirmary.

HEAT

I'll burn autumn waste I've gathered in a heap,
liken the acrid smoke curling into the clouds
unto a wraith I could adopt
if my ascension
were imminent

rake in some more,
and inhale the pall
as if entering the abode
of an under dweller who eschews the light
and tastes darkness on the back of his throat

then, when the flames leap up and devour the leaves,
sense our closeness

to the center

of the earth.

TRUTH SEEKER

Lay me down
to sleep on barbed wire
and I'll know the meaning of discomfort,
caress my lids with a raindrop
and I'll sense the cold,
affix my temple to plate glass
and I'll tell of vulnerability.

When the frost
on the stick no longer clings through the day and night,
the blaze at noon will transfigure the surface
of a pond into a mirror
and reflect into my eye the indefatigable journeyman,
who, just for a week or two,
will play solitaire under the rafters
of a drenched roof

as the pebbles
in the laneway shift with the occasional footstep,
take to the road again
and exclaim:

"I have arrived
at the beginning

although full of verve,
I am not a God."

ON THE OUTSIDE LOOKING IN

Eventually, burnished with the solitary stare
from a concentrated eye, the flower will reveal more
than a blush of purple on soft sheen
or the shadow of an outline
of the object blocking light.

In the indefinite instant congealing a quick thought
and sensitive allurement to Heaven,
one will reveal it is always receptive
to a kiss
from butterfly's wings

and the other, unbeknownst
to its own immateriality,
provide a secure place
to hide from the look that would destroy it
in abundance.

INCONTESTABLE

In twilight, before a very cold, clear night,
when the palaver
is silenced,
an echo from hidden centuries forms like crystals
of ice before my eyes:

Before I admonish the child
who trampled through my flower bed,
I should consider whether his parent carries a knife

before we advance
and rout their defences, we'll send a lone scout
to crawl with ready blade.

When the moon glitters on an iris
I'll pretend it is a living,
real being that illuminates every step
on wayward fields

we'll treasure the guidance
of the stark, white moon,
expecting its luminance
will intoxicate ruminants devouring our hearts.

Between the columns
of ruins I'll lie,
but out of reach of a stone that may fall

when we build this temple,
we expect it will last
for millennia

no portion
will be dislodged,
and the deity to whom we dedicate outstretched fingers
and burnished skin
will breathe hard in judgement
on a future that would position the stars above its brilliance.

BETTER THAN NOTHING

With coarse meal to dry lips
and beads clinking in one hand,
the wanderer would alleviate dependence
on soil, blood, and steam

entranced,
capture gossamer wings
and fly unprotected
into thin air

beyond our reach,
transmute ground meat
into disembodied light,
an opaque horizon into transparency,
pallor into snowdrop white

hunger into emptiness.

I'M ONLY INTERESTED
IN MOUNTAINS AND THE MOON

In the quiet summer's evening
when I see your luminous circular countenance,
I'll catch a glimpse of another height
at the vertex, magnify the mythic Word

the same tone in aural veins
and mile high freshets

unflustered through a flickering eyelid,
abnegate the call
to follow into the clamour and toil,
extricate heat from an outer nebula

a new tempo
on the Arising from the fall
to the bone
and blood of personhood

with lyre of lustrous membrane, beyond interstellar fields
where titans ply thoroughfares circumventing mortality,
and fires illuminate Hyperion's aegis on the far side,
invigorate the Muse's ichor,
enrich a planet with mellifluous chords,
orchestrate fragrance borne
on otherworldly winds swirling from Demeter's abode

heliotrope
and pink tips

out on a limb,
when powdered eyelids mingle in summer blossoms,
caress naked angels
with a brow ballooning large as the sun,
reprise a masterful fugue on bell song lightness,
transmute imagery
into the sound
of desire ripened through chanticleers

out of sight
of Heaven's aura

in isolation, drift outside the capacity
to follow giveness, instantiate forgetfulness,
languish between nothingness of objectlessness
and the ululation without compassion
from the symphony Lucifer treasures

simply,
an excuse to suspend me
from a gantry

far above the crying.

HEAVEN

What do you want?

The same you
only expunged of the peccadillos,
weakness
and desire that makes you you

robed with light
with blazing eyes
enabling you to see the wickedness
of others
and condemn them
to fire

on the footstool of holiness,
forever looking into the aura
of one
who forgives you eternally

on a golden road
in a golden city
relieved of all pain

or a surprise.

I'M ONLY HUMAN

I'll dry my eyes
in the blaze at noon,
offer my feelings to one
who knows why they meld with darkness,
uplift from circumscribed observation
to prescient cognition

realise I am,
as I was, and will be furthermore
on the other side
of darkness where I'll know

but will I want to?

The primrose glowing in dead meat.
Oh, I know why.

The pristine lily flowering from a broken back.
Now, it makes sense to me.

The lucid cloud filtering through torn eyes
and sucked through veins. I get it.

The weight
of this knowledge.

I'd rather not know.

A CALLING

Henceforth,
I shall drink the dew saints brew
when they surrender their blood to heavenly dreams,
eat the manna stored in a wayfarer's knapsack
as he traipses
from one temple to another,
sniff the odor a rose exudes
when the air is crisp
and clear after a rainstorm.

transcendently poised,
build a bridge between calcifying bone nearing its end
and an ear receptive
to the next utterance in nightshade pink,
white
born in invariance,
Archon lit yellow staining the atmosphere
with a mind of its own

disembodied

until the grass tickles my neck.

A LONG WAY TO FALL

Mindfulness shifted shape
and assumed the quality of sunlight bathing the universe,
head high blossoms, as if they were lips,
breathed heavenly fragrance into the atmosphere,
rainbows settled over verdant fields

only a dissatisfied god expecting lesser beings
to idolize distant care for them.

On their usual trajectory,
night ramblers acclimatized ligaments
to unfettered ranges over mystical hinterlands

only the groaning cave of loneliness.

Arbors drifted to parched outskirts,
feathers brushed glossy leaves,
cumulus clouds conquered gravity

only heads bouncing against impenetrable ceilings.

The white robed savant walked amongst us,
healed sores, and attended to the fracture
in our spines

only the request
for sustenance forming rivers
in paradise.

139

HIGH AS I CAN GO

Disinterred deity,
regardless of who brandished the axe,
was the intent to maim
mere avarice to steal your pulse
and leave us on dead ground?
Will the leak from your wound seep into the ill tended plot
on the outskirts of the settlement?
Did the solace
of a comforter issue with your final breath
and flood the rent
in our hearts?

Will the blood from your veins
taste the same as the lucent stretch under sunset,
the layer between sediment and volcanic strata
be edible as your calf muscle?

If so,
we'll join you in harmony
and evince salutation to the higher order
for filling our bellies.

Youthfulness and mastery,
fragility and eternal strength,
witness and execution fused in a repast
the obsessive, the committed,
and the profligate
can suck with their lips.

And who tastes wet open flesh will,
with astral clarity in their sockets,
find firm footing
in lily fields growing outside cerebral encumbrance

the willing to die,
who know nothing precedes utterance
and emptiness comes after,
taste eye gel clearing their sight
and sup at the pool further out
than Hades.

If not a halo transcending a star lit ceiling
and cavernous skull,
at least a whisper calling us to vacate the stale abode

if not vertiginous scales timed with the step
of a goddess who finds her way
to Elysian fields,
at least the clatter of tiny feet retreating from melting orbs
on Doomsday

if not the sing song lilt
of composers enamored with their own melody,
at least a tempo that can be translated into earth speak
a million years
from now

and,
even though the soothing refrain lingering under your skin
may not endure when you have crossed

if,
only for an instant, unstained light

where forgetfulness leaves pain in a furrow.